AND THE

by Dale Lundberg
illustrated by Anthony Lewis

⟨⟨Harcourt
SCHOOL PUBLISHERS

Printed in China

ISBN 10: 0-15-350505-2
ISBN 13: 978-0-15-350505-8

Ordering Options
ISBN 10: 0-15-350333-5 (Grade 3 Below-Level Collection)
ISBN 13: 978-0-15-350333-7 (Grade 3 Below-Level Collection)
ISBN 10: 0-15-357493-3 (package of 5)
ISBN 13: 978-0-15-357493-1 (package of 5)

2 3 4 5 6 7 8 9 10 985 12 11 10 09 08 07

Mr. Enrico announced to his students that they would be having a talent show. The kids in the class were ready to erupt in excitement. Well, all except Bettina.

"I don't think I have any talent," Bettina thought as she sat on the school bus that afternoon.

Bettina's best friend, Alex, sat next to her. "I think that I will play the flute," he said. "What will you do for the show?"

"I'm really worried because I can't think of any talent that I have!" said Bettina.

"Well, can you sing?" asked Alex.

"No, I'm not a very good singer," said Bettina.

"Can you dance?" asked Alex.

"No, I'm not a very good dancer either," said Bettina sadly.

"Don't worry, Bettina," said Alex. "We'll think of something."

That night, Bettina had trouble falling asleep. She thought about the things she was good at. She was good at soccer. You couldn't play soccer at a talent show. She was also good at math. Math was not going to work out either.

Bettina liked to read. She wasn't sure how she could expand reading into a talent. Maybe Mr. Enrico would have some ideas.

After school that day, the kids were getting ready for the show. Kids were singing and dancing, and one kid was even doing karate!

Bettina held her breath. Finally, she went into the room. "Hello, Bettina. What do you plan to do for the show?" asked Mr. Enrico.

"I honestly don't think I have any talents," Bettina said.

"Well, I don't know about that," said Mr. Enrico, "but I have an idea."

Finally, it was the night of the big show.
Everyone was waiting for the show to
begin. The class had done a thorough job
preparing for the talent show. Lisa Larken
was first to go on, and she was going to
sing.

Lisa's song was very nice, but she forgot the words in the second verse. Next up was Roger Hamilton, who was going to dance. Roger did a good job until he tripped and fell halfway through the dance. Everyone clapped anyway, and then it was Alex's turn.

Alex was a pretty good flute player. This time the song was sprinkled with some flat notes. Even so, Bettina clapped and cheered. One by one, the kids got up and performed. Finally, it was Bettina's turn, and she slowly walked onto the stage.

Bettina announced, "I'm going to recite a poem for you called 'Dust of Snow' by Robert Frost."

Bettina did not make a single mistake. Her voice was clear and strong, not grainy or weak. When she finished, everyone cheered. The show was over. Now it was all up to the judges.

The judges' deliberation lasted just a few minutes. "Third place goes to Alex Saunders for playing the flute," said the judges. "Second place goes to Ben Green for playing the drums."

Bettina gathered her things together. She was certain it wasn't possible for her to win.

Then, she heard the judges say, "First place goes to Bettina Johnson for reading the poem."

Bettina could not believe her ears. Mr. Enrico smiled and said, "Being able to speak well in front of a crowd is a real talent!"

"Maybe I have as much talent as everyone else after all!" Bettina said proudly.

Think Critically

1. How does Bettina change during the story?

2. Did you think Bettina would win the talent show? Why or why not?

3. Why do you think Mr. Enrico helps Bettina?

4. What do you think the author wanted readers to learn?

5. Has this story changed the way you feel about what makes a talent? Why or why not?

Science

Snow Facts The poem that Bettina read was called "Dust of Snow." Look up snow, and find out three things about it. Write them down. Then practice saying your snow facts aloud.

 School-Home Connection Ask friends and family members whether they think they have any talents. If so, what are they?

Word Count: 555